Written by: Lisa Bills

Illustrations by: Mr. Sketches
(A.K.A. David Wilson)

Dedicated to my wonderful husband, precious boys and all the fur babies in the house Ellie, Sophie & Bonnie as well as our Chinchilla, Bandit and of course we can't forget Roger, the turtle.

Paperback:
ISBN: 979-8-9927735-1-4

Hardback:
ISBN: 979-8-9927735-0-7

This edition first printing November 2025. Characters (based on true fur babies) and settings created by Lisa Bills, Uppermost Entertainment and published by Uppermost Publishing.

happytailstelltales.com

"Finding Ellie"

AN ADVENTURE *BASED ON*

TRUE EVENTS

I̲T'S an exciting and special day! Mom is picking me up early from School for a special road trip to get my new best friend.

"Hi Blaine!", Said Mom. "Are you ready to find your new best fur friend?

"Yes, Mom! Been praying for it for a long time and so glad today's the BIG day."

"Hi nephew", greeted Aunt Suzy, "it's so great to see you and not looking so blue. This is a very important date!"

"Yes, it is Aunt Suzy" said Blaine, "and I can't wait!"

They quickly arrive at a festival where the dog rescue is located..

"Mom! Aunt Suzy!!
I'm so excited I just can't hide it!"

"We wouldn't want you to! No doubt about it,"
Mom and Aunt Suzy replied.

Blaine asks, "Mom and Aunt Suzy, where's the dog rescue area?"

Aunt Suzy replies, "let's ask the Event Coordinator."

"Sir, Do you know where the animal rescue section is?"

"Oh, yes, ma'am," "Just keep walking straight ahead and y'all will see them on your right."

We arrived at the spot and I couldn't believe my eyes! So many puppies! "Oh Mom and Aunt Suzy." Look at all of these!"

I picked up, Ellie! I just knew she was the one. "Oh, Mom, I want this one! She's perfect!"

Mom, quickly remembering that Dad doesn't have a clue about the new addition to the family, starts to get very nervous and says, "Are you sure, Blaine?"

"Yes, Mom! I'm certain," Blaine replies.

The Rescue Fireman says, "all of these precious pups were rescued from an apartment complex that was on fire and the situation was dire."

Mom seems a little hesitant—Blaine & Aunt Suzy are looking at mom like, it's his puppy and it is, in fact, his choice!

Mom snaps back to reality and realizes it's Blaine's adventure and his choice and gives an understanding agreed look in reply.

The Fireman sensing Mom's hesitation says, "if it's the price, I'll drop it to $20.00 from $40.00."

Aunt Suzy chimes in, "It's definitely not the money."

Mom Says, "No, it's definitely not the money. I'll pay the $40.00. Not a problem!"

14

"Well then," said the fireman, "this furry friend belongs to you young man."

15

"So Blainey," asked Aunt Suzy, "do you have a name for your new fur baby?"

"Well, yes! Actually, I do." Blaine without hesitation, "Her name is Ellie!"

Aunt Suzy says, "Mom, pull over. Ellie needs to go to the bathroom."

Mom turns around and looks at her like how in the world do you know that?

Mom pulls over and Aunt Suzy and Blaine let Ellie out in the field and she does her business.

It's time to pick Dad up from the Dallas train station. Blaine and Mom are brainstorming on how they are going to tell Dad about their newfound furry addition to the family.

Blaine Says, "I know Mom, we'll act like we found her in the field!"

Mom agrees and Says, "that's a fantabulous idea!"

As Dad is approaching, Blaine nervously gets out of the car and lets Ellie out in the grass acting like he's just found her.

Dad asks, "Blaine, what are you doing?"
"I've found a puppy," replied Blaine.

Dad says, "Get away from it, now! Come over here. It might not be safe."

Blaine picks up the pup and Mom and Blaine are looking at each other like we've gotten our hand caught in the cookie jar.

Mom says, "No, she's okay. We actually adopted her today. Her name is Ellie and she's had all her shots and she's the newest addition to the Bills family!"

After several moments Dad finally says, "Well, let's get our newest family member home. We'll enjoy some dinner and fun with our newest addition."

THE REAL ELLIE AND BLAINE

www.ingramcontent.com/pod-product-compliance
Lightning Source LLC
Chambersburg PA
CBHW041604120626
46551CB00002B/299